This book belongs to

_____

Paperback ISBN: 978-1-63731-718-1
Hardcover ISBN: 978-1-63731-720-4
eBook ISBN: 978-1-63731-719-8

Printed and bound in the USA.
NinjaLifeHacks.tv

Ninja Life Hacks®
by Mary Nhin

Ninja Life Hacks®

SHAPES

By Mary Nhin

A ninja knows all about shapes,
From a triangle to a square.

A ninja is able to recognize shapes,
Here, there and everywhere!

Problem-Solving Ninja creates a **square**,
A puzzle with 100 pieces.

Hangry Ninja points out the **circles**,
While making pepperoni pizzas.

Love Ninja uses **hearts** to fly,
Floating all the way up to the sky.

While Focused Ninja spies an **oval**,
Through a magnifying glass eye.

Money Ninja envisions **rectangles**,
Drawing them in the sand.

Smart Ninja thinks of **heptagrams** and **hexagons**—
Which are hard work to understand.

Motivated Ninja sees a **Triangle**,
On top of the rocket the ninjas hold.

Confident Ninja notices a **Trapezium**,
As a shiny super cape unfolds.

Supportive Ninja cheers on Angry Ninja,
Playing baseball on a **diamond** field.

Brave Ninja holds up a **kite** shaped weapon,
Which happens to be a shield.

Positive Ninja stares at the **crescent** moon,
Wondering what could be one day.

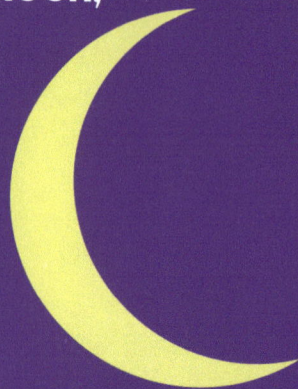

Grateful Ninja recognizes a **pentagon**,
In the envelope they send away.

Creative Ninja draws **parallelograms**,
Including them in a piece of art.

Organized Ninja notices **ellipse**-shaped eggs,
In the grocery shopping cart.

Kind Ninja looks at the **stars** in the sky,
After doing something kind.

Emotionally Intelligent Ninja,
Sees all sorts of **shapes** to find.

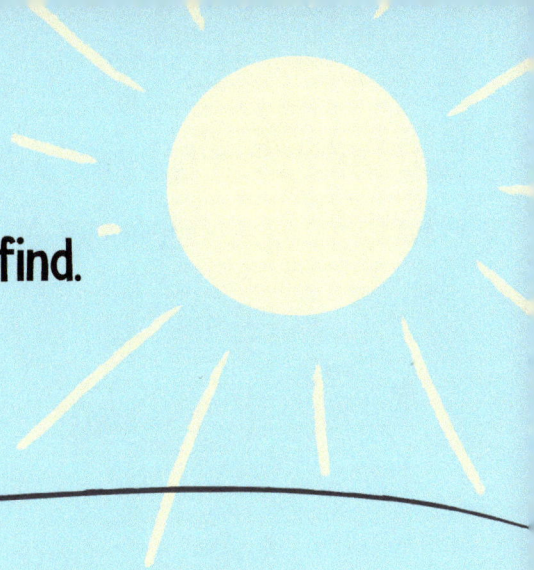

Impulsive Ninja sees an **octagon** stop sign,
But keeps running and ignores it.

Healthy Ninja sees the jump rope make an **arc**,
And uses it to stay healthy and fit.

"Look! Let's figure out this Rubik's **cube**!"
Says Curious Ninja to a buddy.

Memory Ninja's **cylinder**-shaped telescope,
Is great for helping her study.

Grumpy Ninja gets extremely moody,
When there are bad marks.

Helpful Ninja's **arrows** help others,
Stay away from the sharks.

Each ninja loves to look for **shapes**,
As they go about their day.
Because everything around us has a **shape**,
And is unique in its own special way!

SHAPES

Square

Circle

Heart

Oval

Trapezium

Diamond

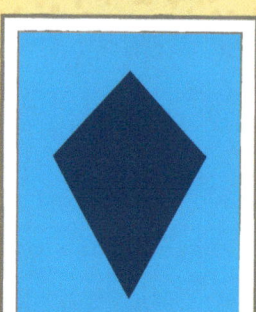
Kite

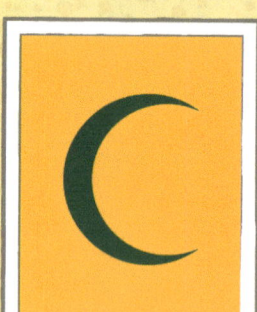
Crescent

Octagon

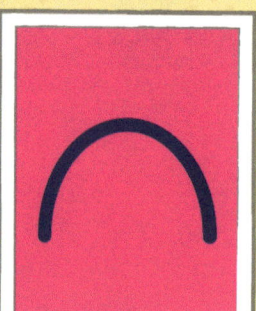
Arc

Cube

SHAPES

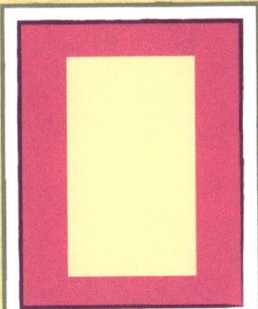
Rectangle

Heptagram

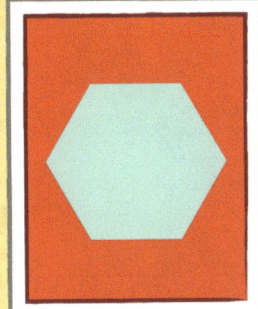
Hexagon

Triangle

Pentagon

Parallelogram

Elipse

Star

Cylinder

Cross

Arrow

Continue the learning with our fun lesson plans which include superpower skills practice, STEM activity, craft, and more! Visit ninjalifehacks.tv

📷 @marynhin @officialninjalifehacks
#NinjaLifeHacks

▶️ Ninja Life Hacks

f Mary Nhin   Ninja Life Hacks

♪ @officialninjalifehacks

www.ingramcontent.com/pod-product-compliance
Lightning Source LLC
Chambersburg PA
CBHW042025090426
42811CB00016B/1741

9 781637 317204